IDIOPHONE

IDIOPHONE

AMY FUSSELMAN

COFFEE HOUSE PRESS

Minneapolis

2018

Coffee House Press books are available to the trade through our primary distributor, Consortium Book Sales & Distribution, cbsd.com or (800) 283-3572. For personal orders, catalogs, or other information, write to info@coffeehousepress.org.

Coffee House Press is a nonprofit literary publishing house. Support from private foundations, corporate giving programs, government programs, and generous individuals helps make the publication of our books possible. We gratefully acknowledge their support in detail in the back of this book.

LIBRARY OF CONGRESS CATALOGING-IN-PUBLICATION DATA

Names: Fusselman, Amy, author.
Title: Idiophone / Amy Fusselman.
Description: Minneapolis : Coffee House Press, 2018.
Identifiers: LCCN 2017040748 | ISBN 9781566895132 (trade pbk.)
Classification: LCC PS3606.U86 I35 2018 | DDC 813/.6—dc23
LC record available at https://lccn.loc.gov/2017040748

PRINTED IN THE UNITED STATES OF AMERICA
25 24 23 22 21 20 19 18   1 2 3 4 5 6 7 8

For Frank

IDIOPHONE

I.

1.

I can't sleep in this uncomfortable New York City cab.
It keeps moving.
It's like the bed in *The Nutcracker.*
You can't sleep in it, you can only pass out in it.
Plus, it's on a battlefield.
I am tired of battlefields.
I am tired of going to sleep like I'm in a war.
I am tired of fighting to do what I want.
I am tired of fighting to do what I want and then fighting
to sleep.
I want it all, boy.
I want to drink a beer.
I would so love to drink a beer.
I had my last beer over twenty-five years ago.
I can't drink a beer now and sleep.
I can't drink a beer now and fight the good fight.

I don't want to read or write about the fight between drinking and not drinking.

I want to read about what people do after they stop fighting that fight.

I want to read about a woman parking her fluffy white bed at an odd angle and leaving the motor running and dashing into the deli to get a coffee light and sweet and then coming out and driving her bed down the West Side Highway with the lace bed skirt flying and the bed pirouetting in the snow.

I want to be still like the world in snow.

I want to be still like the wooden nutcracker I saw backstage at Lincoln Center, standing on the shelf beside his identical brothers.

I didn't know the nutcracker had identical brothers, but when I saw them together it made perfect sense.

More nutcrackers are needed in case one gets broken.

One always gets broken.

I want to be still and not break.

I want to be still and multiply.

I want to see double and triple because I am quadruple.

I want to quintuple.

I want to sextuple while I sit on a throne watching candy and coffee dance for me.

I want to do what I want in a world that does not seem to want me to do what I want.

I want to not have to fight.

I want my mother to stop rabbit-punching me from the assisted-living center in Tampa.

I want my mother to stop reaching her skinny ninety-
year-old arm across the country to rabbit-punch me in
my sleep.

I want to sleep a sleep that's like snow.

I want to be safe and warm like a rabbit in a hat.

I want to be safe and warm in a hat listening to my magician
intone, and then I want to come out of the hat with his soft
gloved hands on my ears and the light all around me.

I want to be in a circle of light that is not moving, that is
protecting me.

I want to feel the world move, every bit of the world,
which is always fighting to live.

I want to get out of the cab and walk up the steps and
stand in the light of the doorway with my key out.

I want to open the door and get out of this world.

I want to get out of this world that is always at war.

I want to get out of this world that I haven't been drunk in.

I want to drink in a new world.

I want to drink in a world that has colored lights and music
like a holiday party.

2.

The most impressive dancer in *The Nutcracker* is the
tree.

The most thrilling part of *The Nutcracker* is when the tree
grows to the music.

As the tree grows, the set changes:

what was once a home decorated for a holiday party becomes a battlefield.

It is so unbelievably easy for one world to turn into another.

In my backstage tour of *The Nutcracker* at Lincoln Center, I saw the giant tree as it was being folded up for a new performance.

The tree is like an accordion that sits in a box under the stage until it's time for it to grow.

When the moment in the music comes, wires pull it up to the ceiling and it unfolds in its glory.

As I watched the tree being compacted, I was sprinkled with some of its snow.

The snow was made of small, iridescent paper circles.

I put a bit in my coat pocket and kept it there all winter as a lucky charm.

I would put my freezing, gloveless hand in my pocket and feel the snow and think, *Ballerinas stepped on this,* and that thought would almost warm me.

The stagehand taking the tree down told me that sometimes the ballerinas slip and fall on the snow.

In the ten-plus years I have been going to see *The Nutcracker* at Lincoln Center, I have never seen a ballerina slip and fall.

I stood and watched the tree until it was completely in its box.

I stood and watched the tree until it was ready to go.

I am in this world, but sometimes I feel other ones pulling at me.

3.

There was a time when I was small and my mother was huge.

There was a time when I was tiny and my mother was huge and horrible and filled with light.

There was a time when parties formed around my mother and shiny boxes were laid at her feet and the windows were opened and closed for her and mice scurried in front of and behind her.

There was a time when trombone slides would glide up and down in skittish ecstasy when my mother walked down the street.

Now my mother is frail.

Now my mother is getting smaller.

Now my mother's bed is moving and she cannot sleep.

It is so unbelievably easy for one world to turn into another.

4.

For a long time I admired *The Nutcracker* simply because of its storyline, which, from my viewings, I understood to be this:

Marie's family has a holiday party.

Marie's magic, eye-patched Uncle Drosselmeier comes and gives her a toy nutcracker.

Marie's brother, Fritz, breaks the toy nutcracker.

Marie is upset, and after the party she goes to sleep with the broken nutcracker in the living room.

Uncle Drosselmeier comes and fixes the nutcracker while Marie is asleep.

Uncle Drosselmeier leaves.

Everything becomes awake.

The Christmas tree becomes gigantic.

The toy nutcracker becomes Marie-size.

Marie-size mice scurry around the living room.

The Marie-size Nutcracker, along with Marie-size toy soldiers, a Marie-size bunny-drummer, and Marie herself, battle the Marie-size mice.

Marie throws her shoe at the king of the mice, which creates a distraction that enables the Nutcracker to kill the king with his sword.

Marie passes out in a frilly white bed.

The white bed dances.

The white bed dances in a snowstorm.

Marie wakes up.

The Nutcracker reveals himself to be a prince.

Marie and the prince travel to a magical land of sweets.

The Sugarplum Fairy dances for them.

Angels dance for them.

Candy canes dance for them.

Marzipan dances for them.

Mother Ginger dances for them.

Polichinelles dance for them.

Hot chocolate dances for them.

Tea dances for them.

Coffee dances for them.

Flowers dance for them.

Grown-up versions of themselves dance a *grand pas de deux* for them.

Marie and the prince get into a sleigh pulled by reindeer.

Marie and the prince wave to us as they fly off into the sky.

That's it.

That's the end.

I admired this plot.

Why can't more fiction be like *The Nutcracker*?

Why can't more authors just abandon their lumbering storylines halfway through and move on to something more interesting, like dancing candy?

Why do you have to be stuck in a horrible world as it plods to its logical end?

Why can't there be mercy?

Why can't you just leave one world and move into another?

5.

The Nutcracker was first performed on December 18, 1892, at the Imperial Mariinsky Theatre in St. Petersburg, Russia. At the helm was the same group that had done *The Sleeping Beauty* two years earlier: the director of the Imperial Theatres, Ivan Vsevolozhsky; choreographer Marius Petipa; Petipa's assistant, Lev Ivanov; and composer Pyotr Ilich Tchaikovsky.

Vsevolozhsky had wanted to make a ballet based on
E. T. A. Hoffmann's 1816 short story "The Nutcracker
and the Mouse King." The story was challenging to bring
to the ballet stage, however: it contains flashbacks; the
Nutcracker and Marie are cursed and made ugly at points;
and nibbles of fat play a role in the plot.

(Personally, I would very much like to see a ballet in which
nibbles of fat are dancing.)

Vsevolozhsky and Petipa simplified the narrative, also
relying on an adaptation of the story written by Alexandre
Dumas, père. The results of their collaboration were
presented to Tchaikovsky, who worked from their list
of directions.

An example of a directive Tchaikovsky worked from:
The stage is empty. 8 bars of mysterious and tender music.

6.

Two mice are shopping at a department store.
They are driving around in their yellow vw Beetle
convertible.
It's old and not super reliable, but it's a good car for the beach.
The mice have been shopping and are shopping some more;
it's like Christmas.
"What do we have so far?" asks Mouse One, who is driving.

"Cheese, cheese, cheese," replies Mouse Two, peering into the bag.

"We need more cheese," says Mouse One.

"You're right," says Mouse Two, closing the bag firmly.

"I'm tired," says Mouse One.

"Let's take a rest," says Mouse Two.

Mouse One parks the car under a king-size bed in the bed department.

It is summer outside; it is cool under the bed.

The mice nap in the car beside a stream of passing flip-flops.

7.

The Nutcracker as performed by the New York City Ballet at Lincoln Center each holiday season—that is, George Balanchine's *Nutcracker*—was originally created by a small group of white men and is commonly danced today by a larger group of mostly white men, women, and children.

It has been embraced by the dominant demographic in the United States, which is—at this moment, anyway; the fight's not over yet—white and Christian.

The Nutcracker has been remade by legions of ballet companies to reflect different takes.

There have been, among many other variations:
a Harlem *Nutcracker*

a bayou *Nutcracker*
two urban *Nutcracker*s (one set in contemporary
Cleveland, one in Atlanta)
a Southwest *Nutcracker* (with coyotes and rattlesnakes)
a Hollywood *Nutcracker*
a Yorkville *Nutcracker*
a Native American *Nutcracker*
a Frisch's *Nutcracker* (named after the Ohio restaurant
chain that sponsored it)
a chocolate *Nutcracker*
a Bharatanatyam *Nutcracker*
a *Hard Nut* (Mark Morris's brilliant, retro-modern
reimagining!)
a hip-hop *Nutcracker*
a dance-along *Nutcracker*
and
a *Revolutionary Nutcracker Sweetie,* in which Drosselmeier
is depicted as a gay skateboarder whose lover has just
died of AIDS.

8.

In all the years I have been going to the New York City
Ballet's *Nutcracker,* I have never seen a ballerina fall,
but I have observed that the ballet unfailingly gets one
laugh. It's at an odd time for a laugh, at one of the
story's most somber moments: when the Mouse King
dies.

It happens like this: the Mouse King, with his seven heads and seven crowns, has just been fatally stabbed by the Nutcracker. He is lying flat on his back, his arms at his sides, his sword still in hand. The music slows and sputters. The battle is over. It is a solemn scene.

Suddenly the Mouse King jerks into an exaggeratedly stiff position; his hands freeze in mid-claw, his legs in mid-run. He is no longer dead, he is "dead," and in this meta move, he reminds the audience that he is alive and that this is a performance. And the audience laughs at how the Mouse King states, in movement, the obvious, and the audience laughs at how everyone has forgotten the obvious, and the audience laughs at how, with this conscious and choreographed movement, the Mouse King overcomes his death. He lives.

That *The Nutcracker* is thought of as simply a festive holiday ritual is baffling to me. How bold is a work of art in which we laugh at death? How bold is a work of art that doesn't tie it all up neatly at the end—that does something, abandons it, and moves on to something better?

The Nutcracker doesn't go from point A to B to A to C to B and back to A in a complicated little dance. It's a straight line: it goes from A to B. It leaps from A to B, really—and the leaps are part of the pleasure.

The Nutcracker, in terms of plot, is structured less like a story and more like a joke. I would argue that this joke organization reflects a human truth that is often danced around: the narratives of our lives tend to end not with a bow but a punch line.

That reminds me: How many mice does it take to screw in a light bulb?
Two, if they're small enough.

9.

I was in the cab with my young daughter.
We had eaten a big brunch, and we wanted to go home and nap.
I'd ordered chocolate-chip pancakes and a glass of milk for her.
I'd ordered a spinach and cheese omelet and a cup of coffee for myself.
She'd only eaten a bit of her pancakes.
I'd eaten some of everything.
The pancakes at this diner are divine;
they are portals to another world.
When they arrive on their giant white plate,
you want to lie down in them.
When you pour maple syrup on them, you can hear angels sing.
You can't just keep going after a meal like that.
You need to pause for a minute.
You need to look back and reevaluate your life.

You need to remember your name and where you are.
You need to remember what you are doing and why.
You need to forget all that, I mean.
You need to forget all that for a while.
And then you need to remember it.
And then you need to keep going.
And then you need to get back into your yellow car and fly
away.

10.

For a long time I didn't think it was a big deal that I blacked
out while drinking.
One time when I was in high school my friend called me
on a Sunday night and asked me if I knew what I had done
the previous night, and I didn't know.
I had thrown up all over the bed in the guest room in her
house, where the two of us had stayed that weekend.
I had done this without knowing, while I was passed out,
and when I got up I still didn't know, and then I had taken
a shower and made the bed and still not known.
I just didn't see it.
My friend wanted me to write a note apologizing to her
mother.
I could have died choking on my vomit; my friend under-
scored this for me.
I wrote the note in longhand on floral stationery.
I put it in the mail and tried not to think about any of it.

My friend's father was the first person I ever met who was sober.

One time as he was driving us home from school he told us how he'd quit drinking.

He had been sober for seven years at that point, which seemed unfathomable to me then.

His wife, my friend's mother, kept a pile of little cards in her kitchen, wrapped up with a rubber band.

They were the kind of cards you include with a bouquet of flowers.

The tower of cards was from all the times he had bought her flowers since he had quit drinking.

The stack must have been five inches high.

It was so exotic to me.

It was like art from the South Pacific on display at the Met.

It was like the slit gong from Vanuatu in gallery 354.

That thing is awesome.

It's over fourteen feet tall and carved from the trunk of a single breadfruit tree.

It depicts an ancestor of the tribe.

It's hollowed out in the middle and has a long, narrow slit that runs vertically down the center.

The slit is its mouth;

the ancestors speak through it.

Slit gongs are in a class of musical instruments called idiophones.

They are a type of directly struck idiophone.

Other types of directly struck idiophones include cowbells,
triangles, and glockenspiels.

I could bang my head on a glockenspiel right now thinking
about my behavior in high school.

I liked my friend's parents a lot.

I was deeply ashamed of myself.

I felt awful about that bed.

It was the bed I was focused on.

It was the bed I clutched in my hand like a crumb.

It was the bed I gnawed and gnawed on in my sleep.

I was racking up stories about not dying in those years.

I was hanging them over my bed.

They hung there, loaded, over my head.

It hurts my stomach to think about them now.

More cowbell.

In college I once walked through a large puddle of gasoline
at the gas station with a lit cigarette in my hand.

I was buzzed and had my headphones on, blasting music.

The guy who was standing by the gasoline tanker truck
next to the spill was yelling and waving at me frantically.

I didn't understand.

I walked through the puddle.

I must have been walking on air.

I must have been flying in a sleigh.

I must have been going to see Santa.

After I cleared the puddle, it dawned on me.

I understood what the puddle was and why he had gestured
so wildly.

I stopped in my tracks for a second.
He looked at me sadly and shook his head.
I was horrified but pretended it was nothing.
I kept going.

I had a couple more years of drinking in me after that.
It's really not all that easy for one world to turn into
another.
I don't know why we are stuck in a horrible world as it
plods to its logical end.
I want to open the door and get out of the world.
I want to open the door and let more worlds in.
I want to be in two worlds at once.
I want to be in three and four and five worlds at once.
I want to sextuple my worlds.
I want candy and coffee to dance for me.
I want the ancestors to speak through my slit.
I want to transmit their message like Tchaikovsky did.
I can't believe how he was working near-blind while
composing *The Nutcracker.*
*The Christmas tree becomes huge. 48 bars of fantastic music
with a grandiose crescendo.*
That's what Tchaikovsky was working with, friends.
That's all that guy had to go on:
just a few words.
How he ever made those sounds, I don't know.
I want to know what he had to guide him.

11.

The New York City Ballet production of *The Nutcracker*
has been a holiday staple in the city since its opening on
February 2, 1954. The ballet begins with the following
image: two children, Fritz and Marie, face us, fast asleep
before a closed door. They wake up and turn around
to look through the door's keyhole. Through that tiny
opening they spy their parents preparing for a holiday
party. They scuffle with each other, trying to catch a
glimpse.

This is hardly an auspicious beginning for a ballet: two
children, first asleep, then tussling with their backs to us,
vying for glimpses of action that we, the audience, can see
only hazily, through a scrim. Yet with this initial image of
two small just-awakened people, scrapping to get a peek
of another world, we begin a journey in which we observe,
and ultimately take part in, a joyful and dramatic enlarge-
ment of vision.

(This theme of expanded vision is emphasized through
the fact that Marie and the Nutcracker-turned-prince
spend almost the entire second half of the ballet—after
the tumultuous battle—as exalted observers. They don't
actually do any dancing; they just sit. Yet they provide a
crucial visual counterpoint: Marie and the prince watch
the same parade of dancing sweets we are watching, only
from the opposite side. An important aspect of the second

act is that we, the audience, are able to watch them mirror our watching.)

By the end of *The Nutcracker,* we have gone through the keyhole with Marie, traversed the superhighway of the plot, and then emerged, like her, into a final moment of illumination: with the house lights on, with every performer onstage facing every applauding audience member, this traditional dissolution of the boundary between observer and observed in the theater has a greater resonance. We are all, finally, in *The Nutcracker.* We are all together in the bright white light in which everyone and everything is visible.

12.

My mother recently told me she was having some trouble with her eyes. She went to the eye doctor, and the nurse stood her in front of the eye chart with the black plastic lollipop you use to cover one eye.

My mother covered her right eye and read the chart with her left just fine. Then she covered her left eye.

"I couldn't believe it," she said. "The chart disappeared."

The way she told it to me, it sounded like there was a magician with her in the doctor's office. After the trick was over, though, my mother was still in the dark. She still can't see out of her right eye, and she still doesn't know why. She didn't ask the doctor or nurses that day. She doesn't like asking questions. She is supposed to go back to the doctor, and until then, she has constructed her own ideas. That they may be incorrect is not a problem for her. Her ideas are her creations, and she loves them.

My mother is happy with her ideas like a mouse that has happened upon a crumb. The world may seem wild and uncontrollable, but a crumb is not. A crumb makes sense to her; she knows what to do with it. She grabs at it, holds it, and will not let it go.

This is in no way a weakness.

I know well how a mouse can be a king.

I know well how a mouse can terrorize with her seven heads and her fourteen eyes, all of them seeing something wrong.

13.

The two mice wake up from their nap under the king-size bed.
They are at the department store because they are going to get married soon.
They are putting together their wedding registry, which is a bit like writing a wish list for Santa.

They agree that next they are going to look at comforters.

"I want down," says Mouse One.

"I am allergic to down," says Mouse Two.

"Come on, that fake down is awful," insists Mouse One.

"But I'll sneeze!" protests Mouse Two.

Just then my mouse-size mother comes under the king-size bed and joins them.

The mice welcome my mother and offer her some Gouda.

My mother and the mice nibble Gouda together in the vw Bug.

The two mice are in the front of the car, and my mother is in the back.

My mother explains to the mice that she has figured out what is wrong with her eye.

She finally read the literature the doctor sent home with her.

She has the severest type of macular degeneration, the kind that causes the most dramatic and irreversible vision loss.

"If I look out of my right eye now, I can't see," she says to the mice.

"That's scary," says Mouse Two.

"Did you choose your china yet?" my mother asks.

"Not yet," says Mouse One.

"Let's go look at china," says Mouse Two.

Mouse One starts the car after several tries.

At last they zoom away, looking for china signs.

14.

If everything I ever drank danced for me, dear God.

If boilermakers danced for me.

If beer danced for me.

If bourbon danced for me.

If whiskey danced for me.

If bright green crème de menthe in crystal glasses danced
for me.

If gin and tonic danced for me.

If grain alcohol and punch that tasted like cough medicine
danced for me.

If wine in wineglasses danced the cha-cha.

If wine in boxes danced the minuet.

If wine in thermoses danced the flop.

If wine in jelly jars danced the bump.

If wine in plastic cups danced the pony.

If wine in wine bottles danced the Macarena.

If gin in shampoo bottles snuck into my high school dorm
did the slide.

If wine coolers shimmied.

If whiskey sours did the wobble.

If daiquiris nodded in time.

Dear God, you know where I am going with this.

You know the punch line already.

If long island iced teas at a joint in Ohio called the Travel
Agency.

If airplane bottles in cars.

If poetry with wine and cheese.

If no poetry and no cheese, just wine.

If they all danced for me.

If magic, eye-patched Uncle Drosselmeier visited me in my sleep.

If he turned his screwdriver.

If he drank his screwdriver.

If he left me sleeping there.

If he left me to spin in my bed.

If everything became awake.

If everything screwed in a light bulb.

Why aren't we dancing? is a really good question.

We should all dance with our drinks.

We should all Marie-size ourselves and dance with Marie-size beverages.

We should all drink what Alice in Wonderland drank and become big and small.

Alice's bottles said *Drink Me.*

Every bottle said *Drink Me* to me.

I don't drink anymore.

I don't know how some days.

I was a kid when I drank and now I'm not.

I was a kid who called beer "liquid bread."

I was a kid who called bloody marys "liquid pizzas."

I was a kid who had what you might call a "carb face."

I had cheeks so chubby that when I smiled you couldn't see my eyes.

I had chubby cheeks like a mouse.

I was storing things in there.

I had compact cars in my cheeks.

I was going places.
I was walking through gasoline with fire in my hand.
My head was an idiophone then.
It needed to be directly struck.

15.

My mother and I recently had a big argument on the phone.
I really let it rip.
I tore a hole in the scrim.
A few days later this thing came up with her eye.
I know I did not give my mother her vision loss.
We fought; she has an eye that went black on her.
It's not related.
The black eye and our fight are not brothers.
The black eye and our fight are not sisters.
My mother and I fight, and it's not a family.
A fight is not a family.
Half the time you can't even see it.
We fight in the air between New York City and Tampa.
We fight in the air over North Carolina.
We fight like the Wright brothers flying on the beach at Kitty Hawk.
We take turns like the Wright brothers flying that crazy machine we built together in the bicycle shop.
We take turns like the nutcracker brothers standing together backstage.

We take turns like the nutcracker brothers going into the spotlight.

We take turns like the nutcracker brothers being broken and being fixed.

I sometimes don't even know if we are battling or not.

Sometimes a battle can be eating lunch with your mother.

I think she is battling as she wheels her walker past the people who are supposed to assist her with living.

I would like to be assisted with living.

I wish I had a mother who was a humongous, lit-up tree.

I wish I had a mother who was an unarmed bunny-drummer.

I myself am a mother,

and I know how hard it can be to mother.

I am a mother who is a tree or a rabbit or a small iridescent paper circle, I don't know.

I don't know what I am anymore.

I ate a stack of pancakes as big as my bed, and now I forget.

I need to lie down.

I need to lie down in the snow.

I need to message Tchaikovsky.

I need to message Tchaikovsky about having almost nothing to go on,

just a few words.

I need to message Tchaikovsky about how annoying it is that words are not music.

It really is not very easy for one world to turn into another.

I do not tell my children too much about other worlds.

I just join with them in the idea that this is the world and
it's solid and it's stable and it doesn't fall apart or disappear
or move.
It's not changing.
This world is not changing, children.
Don't change the world.
I take my three children to Tampa to see my mother, and
we all agree on the idea that we are a family eating lunch
and that this is not a battle.
We sit at a big round table in the assisted-living dining room.
When I see them all together, it makes perfect sense.

16.

My mother and the mice are not having much luck finding
china, so they decide to stop at a bar.
The bar is in the rough part of the department store, near
the camping equipment.
My mother and the mice are drinking boilermakers.
The mouse-size people in the bar do not like the mice with
my mother.
The mice with my mother are of indeterminate gender.
They might be men and they might be women,
it's really hard to say.
While this is generally unremarkable for mice in a drama,
it's less readily accepted by people in the world.
When the news comes out in the bar that these two mice
are getting married, a mouse-size guy tells the mice with

my mother that they need to leave; this bar won't serve them.

The mice with my mother are used to this, unfortunately.

The mice with my mother do not want any drama, so they leave.

But my mother is drunk and wants to fight.

My mother has had only one boilermaker, but that is still one too many because she is a lightweight.

My mother breaks her beer bottle over the head of the mouse-size guy and then runs out of the bar.

The mouse-size guy is on the floor, bleeding.

The mouse-size guy's friends run after my mother.

The mice with my mother are starting the Bug so they can circle around to pick her up.

Mouse One finally gets the Bug started.

My mother is running like hell toward the Bug.

My mother dives into the back.

The Bug takes off like a rocket.

Mouse One is driving the Bug with their heart in their mouth.

It must be hard to be queer in a world that does not want you to be queer.

Tchaikovsky was reportedly gay and was reportedly terrified that this fact would be discovered.

There is some dispute over whether his death at age fifty-three was from cholera or was self-inflicted because his sexuality was about to come to light.

Imagine preferring death over having your whole self come to light.

Imagine that much terror.

Imagine being a rabbit in a hat and being scared to death
of the magician's gloved hands hovering over your ears,
equating the word *abracadabra* with the word
annihilation.

Imagine how small your world would be if you feared any
magic whatsoever:

your entire life deep down inside a black hat.

I wonder how the world would sound, living like that.

My mother and the mice are speeding down below, where
you can't see, through the department store.

Suddenly Mouse One, who is driving, swerves to avoid an
oncoming scooter driven by a drunken cockroach.

Their car crashes into the leg of a dining table.

Everyone is hurt; my mother is thrown from the car.

The drunken cockroach's scooter fishtails but miraculously
keeps going.

Look, it is starting to snow.

When we see static on TV we call it snow.

Writing is not TV.

TV and writing are fighting during my lifetime, it seems.

TV and books are fighting, I should say.

TV and movies and books are fighting, I should say.

TV and movies and books and the internet are fighting,
I should say.

It's not a real fight; it's a fixed fight.

People go see it anyway.

My son tells me this writing business is on its way out.

My thirteen-year-old son tells me books are gonna be ко'd
soon and I better find something else to do.
Every child I've ever met loves a good fight with his mother.
And to go and sit on the couch afterwards.
And to eat snacks and have a cuddle.

II.

1.

When who you are is an affront to other people,
when your way of being is an affront to other people,
when your way of writing is an affront to other people,
when your writing about a particular subject is an affront,
when your voice being heard is an affront to people, the
people with the dominant voice,
the people whose concerns are not yours, the people who
think you should write about *x* and not *y*, the people who
think great art should be about important abstract ideas
and not mice and their problems,
to this I say: fight.
You just have to fight.
You just have to get in there with the unarmed bunny-
drummer and fight.
You just have to get in that *Nutcracker.*
Just get in that goddamned ballet already.

Just drink from the drink-me bottle, size yourself up, and
get in there.

No one ever said it was going to be easy.

No one ever said this world was going to be all dancing
Polichinelles and Mother Ginger.

You know another name for *The Nutcracker*?

I'll tell you another name for *The Nutcracker*.

It's *The Ballbuster*.

I have had my balls busted, I tell you.

I have had my balls busted by mice rejecting my work.

I have had my balls busted by mice who say, "This is a
problem:

your writing is not short stories,

it is not a novel,

it is nonfiction but it is not the kind of nonfiction we are
used to,

it doesn't sound like poetry.

Just put it in a box, would you?

Just put it in a box so we can contain it?"

I have heard that over and over,

like a mouse fight we love to watch each holiday season.

"As an artist, I am a powerful person. In real life, I feel like
the mouse behind the radiator," said my mouse-mother,
the artist Louise Bourgeois.

My real mother was also an artist.

My real mother also busted my balls.

My real and mouse mothers made art, and I write, and
writing busts my balls.

I am having my balls busted right now as I write this.

I am using my hands to write this on the computer as my
balls are being busted.
We don't usually think of writing as a handicraft.
We don't usually think of writing as something like crochet
or knitting; that is, as women's work.
Writing is work a woman has to fight to do.
I wish that fight were through.
I wish women's work were always legitimate.
I wish we could lie down in a fluffy white bed with the
feminized-work fight.
I wish we could take a nap in a cab on that issue.
But that's not the way it is, my loves.
You can't fall asleep.
You have to wake up.
You have to drive your bed-car around the stage.
You can't pass out in battle.
You have to fight to get those words out of your nutcracker
heads, daughters.
You have to get your hands on the keyboard and get those
words out.
And then you have to put that work in the world, which is
so often closed to you.
You have to open that world.
You have to open that world up with your words-sword.
You have to make a slit.
You have to fight your words in there.
You have to fight your words out there.
Imagine your hands on the keyboard:
two mice scurrying around the feet of your mother.

"I worked with my hands," my mother said to me on the telephone during our fight, almost like an apology.

The unsaid thing in that moment was that I do not work with my hands.

The unsaid thing in that moment was that I work with my head, and my hands are my handmaidens.

My hands just flutter around the couch, bringing snacks.

In that moment, her hands were not dominant over my head.

My head was winning that fight.

My head was having its hand raised by the referee at the end of our boxing match.

My seven heads with seven crowns were in charge then.

The pointy ends of my seven crowns were scratching my mother's hands like a cat.

My mother and I never stop battling.

It's hard to stop battling when you don't know where you stop and your beloved begins.

My mother and I were once in the same body.

My mother once held me in her womb.

She once fed me through a cord in her womb.

We danced like that for nine months.

I think of this, sometimes, when I look at my mother: *I came out of her body.*

I think, *There she is: my portal.*

There she is: the door.

Look, here in my pocket.

Ballerinas stepped on this.

2.

The Nutcracker was an E. T. A. Hoffmann story, and then a story by Alexandre Dumas, père, and then a ballet by Vsevolozhsky, Petipa, Ivanov, and Tchaikovsky. And then they told two friends, and then they told two friends, and then it was a ballet by many other people with all sorts of stuff in it like rattlesnakes and crawfish and gay skateboarders.

The Nutcracker is a game of telephone. We used to play telephone in kindergarten. You sit in a circle, and one kid whispers a long sentence to the kid next to them, and then that kid whispers it to the kid next to them, and on around the circle, and then you compare the sentence from the first kid to the sentence from the last kid, and it is funny to hear the differences.

The sentence is always changed from what it was in the beginning, and the way it is changed is something to marvel at.

It's a game about a sentence in which a sentence transforms.
It's a game about a sentence in which a sentence is free to change.
It's a game about a sentence in which the words have no single author.

It's the very first sentence and the very last sentence that you compare side by side.

It would be interesting to see every single one of the sentences written down and laid out in a long line.

You could see the little changes in each one; you could trace the steps from beginning to end.

It would be like watching a dance piece in which the words were the dancers.

Telephone is not a game about a single person having an important idea.

Telephone is a game about the movement of ideas and the movement of language across and through people.

Telephone isn't about one all-important writer flapping their handmaiden-hands alone in a room.

Telephone requires a bunch of people sitting in a circle.

It requires people talking to each other and listening to each other and making mistakes and examining them.

It requires a slender opening like the one in a fourteen-foot-high slit gong.

It requires the absence of a single territorial author-mind.

It invites the ancestors to come and talk.

It invites them for a witnessing.

The telephone game is a witnessing.

The telephone game is a monumental tree in the middle of a party.

The telephone game sees everything.

The telephone game has a twinkly star like a lampshade on its head, and it knows, and it doesn't care.

It just shines.

3.

I interviewed the choreographer, dancer, and director
Annie-B Parson.
I asked her:

>Why do you think so much theater eschews dance?
>Is it related to the idea of what words are and do?

She replied:

>The separation of dance and theater—this is a life long
>irritant for me! In my personal and very subjective
>time line, the distrust in Western theater of dance all
>began post-18th c. Since then, we audience(s) have
>been increasingly subjected to mind-numbing, largely
>un-ironic, unambiguous "reality" on stage. The plays of
>the Ancients, 2000 years ago, were all danced and sung;
>in Shakespeare's time, the actors danced; in classical
>Japanese theater the acting students begin with years of
>dance training. Our contemporary body-less, dance-less
>theater—it feels fear based. Is it related to our Victorian
>fear of the body, fear of corporeality, of sex and death?
>Does the divorce stem from our bias of mind over
>body, rather than mind/body? But yes, the separation
>must have also to do with the modernists' hierarchical
>crowning of the primacy of "the word"; the modernists
>held the word as valuable and honorable, while poor
>dance was considered tawdry, the work of whores

and . . . women! The things that dance owns: ambiguity, layer, mystery, abstraction, the non-narrative—these are the work of the devil! They hide, they suggest, they imply, they don't have an implicit morality or any answers. So, in my tiny corner, I have tried to resurrect dance in theater. Dance is the sacred object for me; it is to be held close and protected from harm, and restored to its rightful place in the pantheon of materiality.

4.

My mother was thrown from the Bug.
She is lying facedown on the floor now.
She has her arms at her sides.
It seems that her shoulder has been broken.
I hope it can be fixed.
The floor is covered in industrial carpeting, a type of floor treatment "which offers stain resistance and durability for places with extremely high foot traffic."
Mouse One is slumped over the steering wheel, unconscious.
Mouse One was wearing their seat belt, but they were also the closest to the point of impact—that is, the dining table leg.
Mouse One's head is bleeding.
Mouse Two's left arm is broken.
Mouse Two is trying to use their right arm to call 9-1-1.
Mouse Two is moaning as they make the call.

The drunken cockroach who was on the scooter and who caused Mouse One to swerve has driven off.

It was a hit-and-run.

There's an awful lot of drinking and driving going on at the department store.

You'd be surprised to know what is going on under your feet, my friends.

You'd be surprised to know of all the traffic under your traffic.

You'd be surprised to hear the conversation in the static.

Things look pretty bad for my mother and the mice right now.

Maybe this is one of those times when we despair over the world we happen to be in.

Maybe this is one of those times when we think how we hate this stupid *Nutcracker.*

Maybe this is one of those times when we think how we hate this stupid *Nutcracker,* which we love and which we buy tickets to every year.

Is there no way out of this *Nutcracker*?

Is this *Nutcracker* always going to be so demanding?

Do we have to remake the goddamned *Nutcracker* in order to get out of it?

Do we have to make our own personalized *Nutcracker* in order to feel like we are in the right world?

The Nutcracker has bodies in it, and bodies always state the truth.

Bodies are miracles that cannot lie.

Bodies lying in and out of cars state the truth.

Bodies lying in and out of beds state the truth.

Bodies lying and waiting for ambulances are truth.

All bodies everywhere are truth.
Mouse Two has managed to call 9-1-1 and now the sirens are screaming.
My mother is still unconscious.
Mouse One is still bleeding, out cold.
There is no bed for my mother on the industrial, stainproof carpeting.
There is no music.
Or there is music, but we can't hear it.
It is very moving and beautiful music.
The stage is empty. 8 bars of mysterious and tender music.
I mean, listen to that.

Those are a few words for you to go on.

5.

Tchaikovsky was in Paris, traveling to America, when he learned that his favorite sister, Sasha, had died. He was supposed to be composing *The Nutcracker* but had been having trouble with it. After Sasha's death, he was grief-stricken.

"Today, even more than yesterday," he wrote to his brother after hearing the news, "I feel the absolute impossibility of depicting in music the Sugar Plum Fairy."

The Nutcracker was one of two projects Tchaikovsky was working on at the time. The second project was an opera.

Vsevolozhsky, the director of the Imperial Theatres, had
commissioned this two-part assignment: *The Nutcracker*
and *Iolanta*.

The libretto for *Iolanta* was written by Tchaikovsky's
brother Modest. It was based on the 1845 Danish play
Kong Renés datter (King René's Daughter) by Henrik
Hertz. The opera premiered on the same evening as *The
Nutcracker* in December 1892, the first half of a double
bill. It was a late night for the mice.

Iolanta, a princess, has been blind since birth.
She doesn't know she is different from other people and
doesn't know she is a princess.
She lives in a beautiful garden in ignorance.
Her father, the king, insists that she must never learn that
she is blind, nor should her betrothed,
Duke Robert.
A doctor visits Iolanta and tells the king that she can
be cured, but only if she is prepared to accept her own
blindness.
The doctor sings a song about two worlds.
The king refuses treatment for his daughter.
Duke Robert arrives at court; he doesn't tell the king, but
he doesn't want to marry Iolanta anymore.
He has fallen in love with another woman.
He and his friend Vaudémont sneak into the garden where
Iolanta is sleeping.
Their sneaking in there is forbidden.

Seeing Iolanta, Vaudémont falls in love with her and refuses
to leave her.

Duke Robert fears she is a sorceress and goes to gather
troops to force Vaudémont to leave.

Iolanta wakes up.

Vaudémont realizes she is blind; he describes color and
light to her.

Iolanta falls in love with Vaudémont.

The couple are discovered by the king.

The doctor says the treatment may work for Iolanta now
that she is aware of her blindness.

Iolanta is not sure she wants to be cured.

The king fears her desire to see is not strong enough,
so he threatens to execute Vaudémont if the treatment
fails.

The duke returns and admits to the king that he has fallen
in love with someone else.

The king dissolves the marriage contract and gives Iolanta
to Vaudémont.

The treatment works; Iolanta can see.

The kingdom rejoices.

The theme of overcoming obscured vision is present in
both *Iolanta* and *The Nutcracker*.

It's too bad you don't often see them together on the same
bill anymore.

Iolanta hardly gets any production time compared to
The Nutcracker.

It reminds me of twins, when one is dominant.

With some twins, you look at them and you can see the
one who got everything.
But maybe the dominant twin is weaker in invisible ways.
You can't always see a person's strength.
You don't always know how strong a mouse is.
In Antoine de Saint-Exupéry's 1943 not-quite-a-children's
book, *The Little Prince,* the prince has an often-quoted line:
"It is only with the heart that one can see rightly; what is
essential is invisible to the eye."
The little prince could be a twin, or maybe a cousin, to the
Nutcracker.
You could imagine them in a bar together.
You could imagine them drinking boilermakers and
talking about their *travails.*

6.

The drunken cockroach scooter-driver is home.
He is going to sleep in his cockroach-bed.
It's an old futon, but it's functional.
He sleeps under a blue cotton blanket given to him by his
mother.
He curls up under the blanket.
He's a cockroach, so he can't curl very well.
He's lying there.
He is really drunk, so he is not going to sleep soundly.
He is not so drunk that he is vomiting, though.
He is just drunk enough that the bed is spinning.

Hold on to the bed, drunken cockroach friend.
Don't pass out and vomit: hold on.

I am a very lucky person.
I am a very very very very very very very very very very
lucky person.
I am sober today.
I am healthy and have a healthy family.
I am a woman, which can be complicated.
I can screw in a light bulb.
I try not to contribute to the antiwoman culture that I am
surrounded by.
It would be great if I would stop fighting with my mother.
It would be really, really, really great if I stopped fighting
with my mother.
I need to try that sometime.
I need to drink from that drink-me bottle.
I am super-lucky.
Everything in my life could be different.
I could easily be folded up in a box.
I could have paper detritus sprinkled around me.
I could be pulled up to the rafters.
I'm not.
I don't know how some days.
I don't know how I got here;
I don't know how I stay.
My mother and the mice are still lying there.
Finally, the ambulance comes.
It is driven by two white baby bunnies.

White baby bunnies make the best medics.
One bunny is calling another bunny on his radio.
The air is filled with that crackling static that is the sound
of bunnies with radios trying to communicate.
The bunnies are hopping softly toward my passed-out
mother.
You have to plod along in one world until it comes to its
logical end.

7.

Is it possible to die from fighting to put your narrative
forward in a world that does not want your narrative to
exist?
Yes, it is possible.
It is possible to die in prison while awaiting trial.
It is possible to commit suicide in prison while waiting
years for your trial.
It is possible to be totally alone.
It is possible to be totally alone with your words.
It is possible to be completely and utterly alone with your
words like a boat floating under a wasteland of stars
or an old man wandering through the cold, dark night with
a gift.
Why can't you just change your sentence?
Why can't you just stab your words with your sword until
they "die"?
Why are they so important to you anyway?

Why do you have to tell your truth?

You know you are not your body.

You know you are not a body that is imprinted with everything you've ever done.

You know you are not a portal to another world.

You know you are not a holder of your soul.

You are not a soul at all.

You are formless.

You are smoke.

You are a writer.

You leave your body when you go to the page, you know.

We're all equal here, on the page.

We're all disembodied.

We're all just words.

You and me, we're just words lined up obediently.

You're just a few words, and you can change them.

You can just easily change your words.

You can just quickly change your words.

You should just quickly and easily change your words.

You should just love your words and be quiet.

You should just hate your words and be quiet.

You should just be alone in your box.

You should wait to be pulled up out of your words.

Just wait to be pulled up out of your world.

Just wait quietly for some rope to pull you up.

Just wait to unfold to the ceiling in your glory.

Just wait there, o.k.?

Just think about something else for a while.

Just think about some other words.

Just think about who is speaking when you speak.

Who are you—your mother, your ancestors?

Can't all words change?

Can't *annihilation* become *abracadabra*?

Can't we all telephone?

Can't we all just call each other up?

Can't we all just message Tchaikovsky?

Can't we all be broken and fixed?

It is so incredibly easy for one word to turn into another.

I didn't know the nutcracker had identical brothers.

But then I saw them together.

I saw them quadruple.

I saw them quintuple.

I saw them sextuple.

I sat alone on my throne with my seven heads and watched them.

The nutcracker brothers octupled.

They were like the Rockettes in the annual Radio City Music Hall *Christmas Spectacular.*

They were doing the toy-soldier number where they all line up and then all fall down in slow motion.

They have been doing that number for almost a hundred years.

Keep it up, toy soldiers.

Don't drop it.

8.

Me:

> I am interested in your characterization of our current
> bodiless, danceless theater as fear-based. Can you
> elaborate on that, and on the ways in which dance, in
> your view, is positioned in regard to this?

Annie-B Parson:

> Dance addresses matters of space from the perspective
> of the body. When we move our body it is immediately
> warm, sweaty, personal—even the cool, detached
> Merce Cunningham's dance is personal. Or, as
> Cunningham said: "We give ourselves away at every
> moment." Who are we? Look at how we move in
> space: what body parts we chose to isolate, combine
> and engage, and with what temporal and muscular
> quality do we engage them. No acting necessary! We
> give ourselves away at every moment when we dance.
> In dance there is no *pretend*—unless we choose to
> layer *pretend* on top of the truth of the body. Perhaps
> this fecundity of exposure is alarming. And dance
> is sympathetic, meaning the audience's body expe-
> riences a leap when they watch one, experiences a
> jump when they watch one, experiences a hip thrust
> when they watch one. Do we want this? No cover!
> No protection from the rain! And the abstraction—

ambiguity is scary as well because it knocks on the
door to the dark box that we try to shut inside of us.
And our response to abstraction is complicated, and
audiences typically like their theater served up with
a moral ending like Arthur Miller or a flashy leap like
Alvin Ailey. This is the American aversion to complicated thinking. We consumers like when politicians
simplify the world for us—this same mind-set exists
in dance audiences.

9.

My thirteen-year-old son and I are taking a boxing class
together.
They play music there, which we like.
It's really loud.
The instructor has to shout his directions, and even then,
we can't always hear him.
We have to watch other people in class to figure out what's
going on.
Still, the instructor never turns down the music.
That's how important the music is.
The lyrics are not, shall we say, feminist.
There are a handful of women in class.
We've heard it all before;
we're focused on doing the work.
Much has been made about the connection between boxing
and dance.

I think of that when the instructor talks about footwork.
We dance around with our gloves on.
I am the oldest in class; my son is the youngest.
We are partners when it's required.
We tap gloves after doing push-ups.
We jab and hook from opposite sides of the bag.
A huge mural of Joe Louis looms over us.
Joe Louis supposedly said, "There is no such thing as a natural boxer.
A natural dancer has to practice hard. A natural painter has to paint all the time.
Even a natural fool has to work at it."
We work in that class, all right.
Louis also said, "You need a lot of different types of people to make the world better."
I think he was on to something there.

10.

The baby bunnies are carrying my mother and the mice into the ambulance.
My mother has been stabilized and given pain medication.
Her right shoulder is broken.
My mother needs to be assisted with living.
My mother needs coffee and candy brought to her on a tray.
My mother and the mice ride in the ambulance to the hospital.
Their Bug is abandoned; the tow truck will get it later.

My mother and the mice do not talk.
The bunnies attend to them carefully.
The bunnies are male.
EMTs are more likely to be male than female.
Maybe that will change someday.
The hospital is nearby, under the area rugs.
The area rugs are all rolled up.
The area rugs are lying there like a pyramid of downed trees.
The bunnies know their way around this place.

In Balanchine's *Nutcracker,* Drosselmeier bandages the toy
nutcracker with a handkerchief.
He is dressed completely in black, but the handkerchief
is white.
It is like a flag of surrender he pulls from his pocket.
Maybe Drosselmeier gives up at that point,
or maybe it's the Nutcracker who gives up.
He is a nutcracker with the soul of a prince.
But we can't see his soul.

It is supposedly the soul that drives people.
It is the soul that drives the body like a driver drives a car.
We can't see the soul-driver; we can only see the body-car
moving.
The whole thing is very confusing.
We should just close our eyes.

The bandaged Nutcracker is on his way to princedom.
It's all there, but we can't see it yet.

Why we can't see what we need to see in this world, I do not know.

Why is it so hard to see what we need to see?

Why do we need to struggle to do the simplest things?

Why is there always a *grand pas de deux* to be done to survive?

What a miracle it is that a waiter will bring you a big stack of pancakes.

What a miracle it is that a waiter will set them in front of you, warm, and you can pour as much maple syrup on top as you want.

You can do this, that is, if you have the money to pay that waiter.

You can do this if you have the money to pay for those pancakes.

There it is, the money problem.

You have to make the money appear.

You have to be that kind of magician in this life.

The baby bunny who is driving the ambulance almost hits a food truck as he pulls into the hospital driveway.

The food truck is driven by a rat.

The rat squeals as he avoids a collision, then he keeps going.

This baby bunny is unfazed by terrible drivers.

He is an EMT; he doesn't screw around.

As he pulls the ambulance up near the hospital entrance, he says, "You know, the barbecue from that food truck is really good."

"Have you had the pork? It's fantastic," the other baby
bunny agrees from the back.

"That rat can't drive, though," says the baby-bunny driver.

"No one looks where they're going anymore," the other
baby bunny says, getting ready to lift up my mother.

The two baby bunnies are joined by more baby bunnies to
get my mother and the mice out of the ambulance.

There are six bunnies in all, two for each gurney.

All the white bunnies have black radios on their hips.

All the radios begin crackling.

All the radios are staticky.

It's a chorus of static.

It's like all the white bunnies and my mother and the mice
are running around in a snow globe of static.

The white bunnies are taking my mother and the mice
someplace in the static-snow.

My mother and the mice are all on gurneys now.

Suddenly the bunnies change.

Suddenly the bunnies unzip their bunny costumes.

Who knew they were all in costume?

Their white fur coats were just very realistic costumes!

They all step out of their costumes, and their white fur
puddles on the floor like melting snow.

Maybe ballerinas will slip on them.

I hope not.

The bunnies are no longer white bunnies.

Now they are all men in black suits with black top hats.

They are all men in black capes with white gloves.

They are all magicians!

They have black magic wands instead of black radios!
The static has stopped.
The stage is empty. 8 bars of mysterious and tender music.
The magicians wheel my mother and the mice through the
automatic doors.
Wow, this isn't a hospital after all.
This room at the end of the hall where they wheel my
mother and the mice isn't the operating theater.
It's a theater-theater.
That's not to say there are two theaters, but one theater
that is itself.
I underscore its selfhood by saying its name twice.
Maybe we can apply that logic to the idea that this world
is made more world-y by the presence of other worlds.
Maybe we are in a world-world and not just a world.
Maybe our world is larger and more multidimensional
than we are generally led to believe.
Maybe it would be helpful for us to remember this when
the essential things are hard to see.
Maybe it would be helpful for us to remember this when we
are frustrated by our world.
Maybe we should actually just seek to see double all the
time.
Maybe we should actually seek to see triple and quadruple.
Maybe we should go out and seek to be in a world-world-
world-world-world-world-world-world-world-world.
People, meaning mice, are often perfectly happy to keep
the door of their one world closed.
Keep that door shut, dormouse.

Sit in there, in the dark, with a drink.

Now the magicians wheel my mother and the mice to the theater-theater.

Oops, the magician pushing Mouse One is not a very good gurney driver.

He is a bit chubbier than all the other magicians.

He is pushing Mouse One's gurney as he tries to eat a ham sandwich.

He almost rear-ended Mouse Two's gurney.

Watch out, ham-sandwich magician!

Didn't they teach you how to drive in magic school?

My mother and the mice are wheeled onstage.

They are going to be in a magic show!

Oh my goodness, the ham-sandwich magician is getting a saw out!

Is he going to saw my mother and the mice in half?!

11.

In his essay "Winnicott and Music," Nicholas Spice writes that children who learn to play music are frequently taught to respect certain master composers. He uses Mozart as an example.

I am going to quote the passage here, but I am going to change *Mozart* to *Tchaikovsky*. I am going to put Tchaikovsky in a box so he is safe and protected in a world he never asked to be born into.

Spice writes:

> To learn respect for [Tchaikovsky] is to be free to pull
> [Tchaikovsky] to pieces so as to see how [Tchaikovsky]
> is made and where [Tchaikovsky] is well made and
> where less well made. It is to pull and push and stretch
> and bite [Tchaikovsky], to rail against him and say you
> are bored by him, to love him and hate him, to test him
> (if necessary to the limits of destruction), to burlesque
> him and alter him, to steal from him and make him your
> own. To learn to respect [Tchaikovsky] is to discover
> that nothing you do to [Tchaikovsky] will change him.
> That he survives. It is to treat [Tchaikovsky] as a body
> of human knowledge and not as a collection of reli-
> gious texts. To use [Tchaikovsky] as a springboard for
> something new. To encounter him as one composer
> to another.

I called up Tchaikovsky and asked him how he wrote the
majestic, tree-growing music in *The Nutcracker* off the
words *The Christmas tree becomes huge. 48 bars of fantastic
music with a grandiose crescendo,* and he told me that he
didn't look to the director's notes to get the job done. He
didn't look to anything outside himself. He stayed in his
box, he said. He went into the box of himself and stayed
there in the pitch-dark with the door locked. He was free
in there, he said, completely and utterly free.

He told me that. And then he hung up on me.

12.

Light acts as an antiseptic, has medicinal properties, and is
a food for plants and trees.
We go to the theater to be enlightened.
We sit in the dark to watch the stage.
We sit in the dark so we can see better.
We sit in the dark so we can focus on the important things.
It always seems like there are really intriguing things going
on along the sides and in the corners of the tether, though.
I just misspelled *theater* as *tether.*
The theater is a tether.
It ties us together and pulls us in.
Let's hope it pulls us up and doesn't drag us down.
Let's hope it pulls us up but doesn't hang us.

I learned something about Tchaikovsky, I mean, the Talking
Heads: when they first formed, they wrote a manifesto about
their work. One of its stipulations was that they would not
perform in rock-star lighting; that is, with the audience in the
dark and themselves under purple spotlights, with dry-ice
fog, etc. They would perform in full light. They would perform under crappy fluorescent overheads. They would try to
undercut that rock-star mysteriousness. They would be seen
as they were, as humans playing instruments and singing.
They would work against the idea that they should be viewed
as gods. They were not gods.

Of course, they were gods, though.

13.

My daughter and I recently bought a necklace in the jewelry department of a department store.

That is, we bought two necklaces.

There are two necklaces, but the charms on the two necklaces fit together into one charm.

The charms are two halves of a broken heart.

One half is pink and one half is red.

My daughter decided she wanted the pink one.

It says:

MOT

DAUG

Mine is the red one and says:

HER

HTER

When my thirteen-year-old son saw the necklace on me, he said wryly, "Oh, so you're a hurter."

I smiled. My heart was breaking.

I am trying to raise my three children as if we are stable.

I am trying to raise my three children as if we are in a place that is like the place where horses live, in wooden boxes next to wooden boxes.

I love that horses run and make a sound like thunder simultaneously.

I admire the sound of horses running out of their boxes.

I admire the beating of horses' hooves.

Horses' hooves beat the ground as if the ground were a directly struck idiophone.

Maybe they are an ongoing demonstration of this fact.

Maybe the world is actually an idiophone.

More cowbell.

We live in boxes next to boxes in this city, and sometimes the boxes come tumbling down.

The world is terrifying, I am telling you.

It's fighting.

Let's not forget the fighting.

A boxing ring is a box in which a controlled fight takes place.

During fights that are not controlled, a box can seem like a comforting place to go.

Let's hear it for comfort.

Let's hear it for resting in a box with your eyes closed, smiling, as the saw in the hand of the magician hovers over your belly and then finally begins its *grand pas de deux* with the wood, and the little bits of sawdust go flying through the air like snow.

14.

The Talking Heads' David Byrne used to live across the street from us here in New York City. He was one floor below us. If I stood on our porch I could see a little bit into his apartment. I could occasionally see him from his ankles down, walking around.

He had a Christmas tree up all year round. I guess it was always *The Nutcracker* over there.

15.

My mother is onstage, in the spotlight.

She is on the gurney, in a box.

Her head and feet are sticking out of the ends of the box.

She has her eyes closed.

She is smiling.

I didn't know that this world existed, but now that I see it, it makes perfect sense.

The ham-sandwich magician is the magician king—go figure.

He has a big top hat and a female assistant.

He addresses the crowd with his booming voice.

I can see glimmers of spit when he talks.

The ham-sandwich magician takes up a lot of space.

He is holding his shiny saw high in the air.

It looks like he is going to saw my mother.

Mouse One and Mouse Two are offstage.

I hope they are being treated.

The ham-sandwich magician seems very sure of himself.

Magicians always seem sure of themselves.

That's kind of where they have to go with their performing.

It would be interesting to see a magician who acted like he had no idea what he was doing.

I think that's probably the territory where magicians and clowns overlap.

Magicians and clowns are yet another example of two tribes that don't always see eye to eye.

I am just going to sit here and watch what happens.

I am just going to be a patient audience member.

When you sit down to watch a performance it's always a bit of a risk.

You have be prepared for the possibility of a bad show.

When *The Nutcracker* finally premiered in Russia, the critics were not crazy about it.

Some critics wrote that there were too many children in it.

The ballerina who danced the part of the Sugar Plum Fairy was called "a cow."

Tchaikovsky himself had reservations.

He wrote in a letter, "*The Nutcracker* was staged quite well: it was lavishly produced and everything went off perfectly, but nevertheless, it seemed to me that the public did not like it. They were bored."

16.

The Nutcracker, as a ballet, may be a considered a piece of high art, but it is often dismissed as anti-intellectual.

It's merely decorative.

It's not serious;

it's not tragic.

A mouse death is not tragic, people.

A mouse death happens on the floor, under your feet.

Don't look down.

Just don't look down.

Don't go into that world.

Maybe people dismiss *The Nutcracker* because they don't see it fully.

Maybe people see *The Nutcracker* with that black plastic lollipop over one eye.

Sarah Kaufman, Pulitzer Prize–winning dance critic for the *Washington Post*, wrote this in 2009:

> The tyranny of *The Nutcracker* is emblematic of how dull and risk-averse American ballet has become. . . . There were moments throughout the 20th century when ballet was brave. When it threw bold punches at its own conventions. . . . Where are this century's provocations? Has ballet become so entwined with its "Nutcracker" image, so fearfully wedded to unthreatening offerings, that it has forgotten how eye-opening and ultimately nourishing creative destruction can be?

Maybe *The Nutcracker* is not fighting.

Maybe *The Nutcracker* should throw more punches.

Come over here, *Nutcracker,* I need to talk to you.

Come over here to this corner of the ring.

We need to have a serious talk.

According to longtime *New York Times* music critic Harold C. Schonberg, Tchaikovsky's music was "lacking in elevated thought."

I guess that's what happens when you try to do two term papers at once, Tchaikovsky.

I guess that's what happens when you try to finish your
dance and opera homework at the same time there, sir.
You're in too many worlds, Tchaikovsky.
But maybe the problem is not with *The Nutcracker.*
Maybe the problem is that we don't see *The Nutcracker*
clearly.
Maybe the problem is that *The Nutcracker* is a dance poem
about consciousness, and consciousness is boring.
Maybe the problem is that *The Nutcracker* is a dance poem
about enlightenment, and enlightenment is boring.
It's not fighting,
it's sitting under a tree.
Enough with trees and sitting under them, for Chrissake.
Enough with presence under a tree.
Fighting is more fun.
Fighting is more fun unless you're really tired.
I am going to pray right now to the Shiva of coffee.
I am going to pray right now for a double macchiato to
appear by my desk,
and then I am going to drink it,
and then if Santa Claus comes down my chimney I am
going to punch him.
That guy, putting presents on my floor, on my area rugs,
on my carpeting, creating a carnival underfoot.
What's he doing?
Probably can't drive very well, either.

17.

My mother is in the circle of light.
The ham-sandwich magician is Tchaikovsky.
The nutcracker became a prince;
the ham-sandwich magician becomes Tchaikovsky.
That's how things work around here.
That's how things progress in this drama.
Tchaikovsky is going to work on the box with my mother
in it.
He can do this, no problem.
The box with my mother in it is like his piano.
It is the black box on wheels where he keeps his grief.
It is the black Steinway where he keeps his grief over all the
people who have ever been cut in half,
over all the people who have ever been cut off,
who have been in jails and hospitals and mental institutions,
the places where people with drug and alcohol problems
often end up.
He has his shiny saw hovering in the air like a star over
all that.
He is opening and closing the mouth of his expensive
black Steinway puppet to say something about that.
He is opening and closing the mouth of himself, speaking
his full truth in sounds.
He is opening and closing the mouth of his puppet-self
that is not speaking in words, just in a pattern of sounds.
Sounds can be choreographed.
Two mice can screw in a light bulb.

Magicians can appear and disappear.

Everything can be awake.

Author and curator Eric Kjellgren notes in the *Journal of
Museum Ethnography*

that Tin Mweleun, the master carver who made the slit
gong on display

at the Metropolitan Museum of Art,

"employed magic" to do his work.

Before he carved the slit gong, he drank a powerful concoc-
tion of leaves and coconut water.

My guess is there was some fermentation in there.

He also applied leaves to his eyes to make his vision "clear."

To see clearly you have to obscure your vision;

the Talking Heads said as much in *Stop Making Sense*.

18.

Sometimes when I am with my kids I pretend I am a mouse
in *The Nutcracker*.

This is actually not so difficult to do.

I will tell you how to do it.

I will be a magician who breaks the magician rule,

a magician who explains my tricks.

O.K., here's how it goes:

Take your two hands and put them together under your
chin so your knuckles are against your jawline.

Wiggle your fingers energetically, as if you have a wiggly
finger-beard.

Do this while hunched over,
running across your living room in tiny steps.
There—you are a mouse.
There—you are dancing.
And now maybe you are dancing on the bar.
And now maybe you are dancing to cowbells, triangles,
and glockenspiels.
And the ancestors are speaking as you dance.
And the ancestors are saying, *Wow, you are drunk;*
you better go home now.
You better get in a yellow cab.

Tchaikovsky is done sawing my mother.
He is holding the saw out in his right hand, and his female
assistant comes and takes it.
He does not look behind him for the assistant; he just holds
it out and she takes it away.
He withholds his glance from her and yet expects her to
see him.
He expects her to see the saw, and she does.
She is not seen by him, but she sees the saw.
It's amazing how assistants can do that,
how mothers can do that with trays of snacks.
Tchaikovsky sawed my mother in half.
He sawed her, and then he split apart the hinged box to
prove it.
The hinged box of my mother opens differently than the
hinged box of his piano.
The hinges are in different places.

Tchaikovsky opened the box so the sawed parts of my
mother faced him.

He sawed her like she had never been sawed before, and
we all saw it.

My mother is lying there with her eyes closed, smiling.

Only Tchaikovsky can see the sawed parts of her.

He doesn't seem alarmed by what he is seeing.

He is waving his arms around in the air.

It is all very dramatic.

I wish my doctor's appointments were this exciting.

Instead I sit on the table, cold in my robe, while the doctor
intones about cholesterol.

Once you have a body, you're screwdrivered.

Let's look at that for a second.

Let's look down into that world and contemplate that.

Let's not pretend that world doesn't exist.

Presumably Tchaikovsky is going to mend my mother now.

She is broken and now he will fix her.

I wonder what he sees inside my mother?

Maybe there is nothing to see.

Maybe my mother is hollow.

Maybe she is hollow like a hollowed-out breadfruit tree.

Maybe she is hollowed out like a slit gong.

Maybe she was eaten on the inside by mice.

Maybe she was nibbled by her desire to be an artist.

Maybe it was that she never went to college.

Never went to art school.

She grew up on a dairy farm and left home as soon as she
could.

Her forays into art were taken as seriously as they could
be for a housewife without a fine-art background making
ceramics and quilts.

The Cleveland Museum of Art once exhibited one of her
quilts in a group show.

It was one of the highlights of her artistic life.

I recently found out that her ceramics were featured in a
national show with Peter Voulkos.

That was before I was born.

Tchaikovsky is waving his arms over the hinged box with
my mother.

He is waving his arms to music.

When you think about it, that's what pianists do:

they wave their arms to music over hinged boxes.

Did I ever tell you the one about the two mice who walked
into a bar?

You'd think one of them would have seen it.

19.

My mother was a ceramist when I was very young, but
then she moved on to making quilts.

She would show me the quilts she was working on when
I came home from college.

I remember one of them stood upright.

It was twenty-one inches tall and shaped like a four-sided
pyramid.

The pyramid was on casters; it was like a little car.

Its four sides did not meet at the top.

She placed a little flap that opened and closed there, like
the top of a tank.

It was a car/tank/quilt.

She titled it *Construction,* which was pretty safe, I'd say.

She exhibited it in several group shows in Ohio.

It never made the cut for the big national quilt show in
Kentucky.

One of her pieces did, but not this one.

A quilt on wheels was a little out-there for the national show.

It was a little too free-form for that crowd.

There was no *salon des refusés* for the national quilt show.

You have to be at a certain level of art-making to even have
a *salon des refusés.*

But if there were one, I'd say *Construction* would have been
in there.

Should have been, anyway.

Coulda been a contender.

20.

Tchaikovsky closed up the box of my mother.

But right before he was done, he took out her gallbladder.

That thing was inflamed, the assistant told my mother later.

It was inflamed with grief and frustration, she said.

My mother had never had an organ removed before.

She wondered where her gallbladder was taken.

She didn't ask the assistant, but she wondered about it.

She came up with an idea, I am sure.

I know what happened, and I'll tell you:

The drunken cockroach has it.

He is driving the gallbladder-car now.

He doesn't want to be seen on his scooter in case someone wrote down his license plate number after the
accident.

He doesn't want to be charged with a hit-and-run, so he is
driving the gallbladder-car.

It's fast like a hot rod.

The cockroach is still drinking and driving, so I am not
sure how long the car will last him.

Be careful, drunken cockroach.

You don't want to end up like E. T. A. Hoffmann.

That man had a tough time of it.

"Forever a part of his life, heavy drinking and overworking
made Hoffmann's living hard.

He contracted digestive difficulties, degeneration of the
liver, and neural ailments,

the treatment for which was applying red-hot pokers to
the spine,"

reads the North Carolina Academy of Dance Arts's online
history of *The Nutcracker.*

I can understand why a man with digestive difficulties
would write a story about dancing candy.

I can understand why he would write a story with a
magic uncle in it while he was in bed with a wand hovering
over him.
It was a black metal wand with a fiery red end.
Who held that wand over him? I wonder.
Hoffmann reportedly based the Uncle Drosselmeier
character on himself.
Maybe he himself applied the red-hot poker to his body.
He just kept going, poor guy.
He just kept cooking with gas.
He just kept walking through gas with his fire wand.
I wish he could have come to the diner with my daughter
and me.
I think he would have applauded the pancakes.

The bandaged mice are out for a drive now.
They are healing up quite nicely.
They are driving with my mother in her *Construction*.
They can park the *Construction* and close the lid and take
naps and eat cheese in there.
It's more protected than the convertible; plus, the engine
starts the first time.
All in all, it's an upgrade.
My mother and the mice are going to the beach.
Mouse Two has their arm in a cast.
Mouse One has many stitches and a bandage on their head.
My mother is completely healed.
She is driving them all in her quilt-tank.
She is driving them all to Louse Point for a picnic.

She is experiencing postsurgery euphoria.
She is filled with gratitude for her life.
Tall and benevolent trees line the road.
The cockroach is also going to Louse Point, but he is an hour or so behind them.
The gallbladder-car doesn't get such good mileage.
He has to stop at the gas station.
He walks through a puddle of gasoline on his way to the pump.
He is not smoking a cigarette.
It's not a tragedy or an almost-tragedy.
It's filling up the car; that's it.
He fills up and he goes.
He also buys some candy for the road.

III.

It must be nice to put your fingers on a keyboard and make
music.
It must be nice to put your fingers on a keyboard and make
sounds that are beautiful,
sounds that are musical,
sounds that do not sound like drunken cockroaches reciting
limericks,
sounds that do not sound like drunken cockroaches stut-
tering, *Kafka, Kafka, Kafka.*
I try to find something lyrical
when I make these hammered sounds with my hands.
And I wish this extraordinarily odd activity weren't off in
its own world.
I wish words written and arranged by women were valued
as much as words written and arranged by men.

Written words are interesting in that they come from both
brains and hands.

They live between two worlds that way;

they are tricky.

If you are a writer at a keyboard, you have to be a magician.

You have to wave your arms around over your very particular choices.

You have to make sure not to use *abracadabra* when you
mean *annihilation*.

Or you have to be sure of all *annihilation*'s meanings, since,
according to the dictionary, there are two.

The first one you know already.

The second is from physics, and it is "To convert (a subatomic particle) into radiant energy."

I like that second definition.

I want some radiant energy, let me tell you.

I want that all the time when I am trying to do things in the
material world with my hands,

like write or hollow out a breadfruit tree.

I have never hollowed out a breadfruit tree.

I have no idea how Tin Mweleun, master carver, could
hollow out a fourteen-foot-tall breadfruit tree.

But I can't imagine how people's hands do most things.

My hands are like two nibbles of fat, dancing.

The physical world is a constant challenge for them.

I star in my own magician/clown routine every day.

My routine includes spilling stuff all over myself, spraying
food out of my mouth, and dropping and breaking things
constantly:

it's just endless accidents followed by endless cleaning
up.

It's like I should just get dressed every day in a roll of paper
towels.

I should just get up and make myself a toga out of paper
towels.

I should put on my paper-towel toga and walk into a bar.

I should just wear a big white suit like the one David Byrne
wore in *Stop Making Sense,*

except made out of paper towels.

I should just be prepared for spills like that.

Thank God I live in a city where I don't have to drive.

Thank God I am responsible only for standing more or less
calmly on the sidewalk portion of a street corner where
there is only a small risk that some driver or bicyclist will
jump the curb and take me out.

You can hear the cockroaches singing their gratitude right
now.

You can hear them singing praises of my screwing in light
bulbs.

I tell my husband all the time that burned-out light bulbs
are my *bête noire.*

We live in an apartment with many light bulbs,

and every time a light bulb goes out it feels like an emer-
gency to me.

It's like a young, drunk person has passed out in my guest
bed.

It makes me very anxious, like I need some white baby
bunnies immediately.

And invariably I am home alone with this problem, and
the passed-out light bulb is too high for me to reach.
And I have to make some sort of structure out of chairs,
which I then have to stand on,
in order to reach the blacked-out bulb, and my chair struc-
tures are always unsound.
And I myself am always a baby bunny in these moments,
so I can't climb stacks of chairs very well.
They didn't teach me about stacking chairs in EMT school.
They didn't teach me how to climb stacks of chairs like in
the Moscow circus.
So there I am, hoping I am not going to break my neck on
my poorly made tower of chairs.
And then I finally reach the light bulb and try to unscrew it,
and that is always a surgery
I have the wrong instruments for,
like I am trying to hollow out the center of a fourteen-foot-
high breadfruit tree with a melon baller,
and my fingers can never grasp the light bulb securely,
and a couple of times I have done that thing where I try to
unscrew the light bulb
and instead I pull out the glass part but leave the threaded
metal base still in the socket,
like somehow I separate the glass from the base, the two
parts that are supposed to be forever joined.
How I do that, I don't even know.
It's like a miracle I don't want,
which is sometimes what my life is.

And then I am standing there with bits of broken glass
falling on me like iridescent paper-circle snow,
and I hope I am not going to slip and fall like a ballerina in
The Nutcracker,
and there are wires sticking out where I am supposed to
put in the new light bulb,
and I can't touch the wires because I am scared I will electro-
cute myself,
and I know I have to climb back down the chair-tower
carefully,
but for a few seconds I just have to stand there and swear.
I just have to stand there swearing and trying to see the entire
situation like the giant Christmas tree in *The Nutcracker.*
I just have to stand there like my own gigantic-mother
slit gong.
And it is going to be dark forever in this corner of the
apartment, I think.
And I will always and forever be standing in the dark.
And I am huge and horrible and filled with light.
There is a party around me and a star on my head.
And I don't care.
I am alive right then in my furious glory.
I am converting subatomic particles into radiant energy.
I am shining.
You can see me for miles.
You can set your course by me.

IV.

1.

"And now it is finished, *Casse-Noisette* is all ugliness,"
Tchaikovsky wrote when he finished *The Nutcracker.*
Over time, however, he began to love the music he had made.
"Strange that when I was composing the ballet I kept think-
ing that it wasn't very good but that I would show [the
Imperial Theatres] what I can do when I begin the opera.
And now it seems that the ballet is good and the opera not
so good," he wrote.
Nothing is stable, I tell you.
The horses run wild, and so do the children.
More cowbell!

Our friend E. T. A. Hoffmann was still having a rough go
of it;
at the end of his life he became ill with a disease
that gradually paralyzed him,

moving from his feet to his brain.
When he could no longer use his hands to write,
he hired an assistant and dictated
until almost the hour of his death.
Imagine that.
Imagine being reduced to a mouth.
It reminds me of something my friend Melissa told me;
she heard it from a friend whose son performed as a soldier
in *The Nutcracker.*
She said that the ballerinas who dance in the snowstorm
have to keep their mouths shut.
They actually have to clench their teeth or the snow from
the blizzard will fill their mouths.

Imagine your mouth is not your own anymore.
Imagine your mouth is just a slit,
and it won't open and close easily,
and words that aren't your words are put into it.
Artists, you have to battle that;
you have to win that bout.
You can do it; I know you can.
The boxing instructor says things like that to us.
He believes in us; we're like Santa.
At the end of class, he tells us we can rest.
By rest he means, "Do a plank."
He calls this *active rest,*
which is an oxymoron if I ever heard one.

2.

The yellow cab carrying my daughter and me is taking an
unexpected turn.
Now it is flying in the air.
This doesn't bother me; I am excited.
I am excited to find Santa and clock him over this crazy
holiday he has made,
this holiday I have to figure out how to make my own every
year.
Things could so easily be different.
I could be in a different world.
I could be living in Vanuatu.
In Vanuatu, authorship is understood differently.
The person who commissioned the slit gong—in this case,
the tribal chief—is considered its creator.
The carver is just an assistant.
Many artists here work in a similar way.
Jeff Koons and Damien Hirst come to mind—
employing studios to fabricate their pieces.
A million other artists before them have done that, too.
Maybe things are not so different.
Maybe all worlds are the same.
Maybe we're all just in one world.
There's an old saw for you.
I always hated that saw; it's treacly.
And yet in some ways I think that's where we need to get
going.

That's the place we need to head toward—the sharing of
resources and peaceful coexistence.
In that world I would live and share peacefully with
people who think I should not write books,
who think women should be subservient and hidden,
who view my female body itself as a threat.
Yep, that's where we need to go, all right.
We need a map for that.
Maybe you can work on composing a guide for that,
Tchaikovsky.
See what you can do with just those few words,
with *sharing of resources* and *peaceful coexistence.*

I can tell you that flying in the yellow cab in the air over
New York City,
beside my sleeping daughter,
I thought of my mother.
I thought in particular of my mother's *Construction*
and how it was really remarkable
in how it was created.
She'd developed this technique
where she took photographs of her fabric.
And then she put the photos on her worktable
and used a mirror contraption she'd made—
two mirrors, connected with hinges.
She had these mirrors custom cut at the glass-and-mirror
store,
and then she connected them with pieces of clear packing
tape.

She played with photos and mirrors until she found a
design she liked
that was partly on her table and partly in her mirror.
It was like something Copernicus would have done, had
he been a quilter.
Then she cut up the photographs to create a two-
dimensional rendering of the image she had found.
And she made a color copy of that
and transferred the color copy to cotton fabric with
chemicals.
The intricate pattern on the fabric was created via this
process,
and for her to submit this to a national quilt show was an
uppercut to the idea
of quilting as a laborious handicraft done solely with needle
and thread
in order to produce something flat
to be hung on a wall
or laid on a bed.
She rolled her quilt-tank into the square of that.
I don't know how conscious my mother was of the subver-
sion in her *Construction*.
I don't know how many mice of hers were in that light
bulb.
I don't know if she was aware that what she was doing was
sculpture
and possibly conceptual art
in a context that wasn't prepared to accept, much less
embrace, either.

I saw the whole thing as I was flying in the cab over New York City.

I was an exalted watcher.

My mother was stopping traffic like the Rockefeller Center Christmas tree.

She had big, shiny balls on her.

3.

My daughter and my husband recently went to the flea market.

My husband lets my daughter choose one thing she wants there each time they go.

She chose a box covered in red Chinese fabric, worn and a little dirty.

My daughter is obsessed with boxes
and putting things into other things.

They bought the box for five dollars.

Inside it was lined with more fabric
and nestled within the fabric were two metal balls and a piece of paper.

One side of the paper had text written in Chinese and the other side had text written in English.

I read the English side, which was titled "Synopsis of the Healthy Ball."

My daughter picked the balls up to show me that they made sounds when you moved them.

They were something between a bell and a ball.

The paper said they were to be used for exercise:
"The balls are placed in one's hand and rotated in either a
clockwise or counter-clockwise direction."
The point of this exercise was to "keep all of the points in
one's hands in constant motion,"
with "the muscles in one's fingers and forearms contracting
and relaxing harmoniously."
I held the balls in my hands and tried to do the rotations.
I thought my nibble-of-fat hands could do with some
of this.
My hands didn't dance with the balls very well.
But the balls indeed made a pleasant sound,
a high metal tone, not quite like a bell at Christmas.
It didn't have the same tone.
It was slightly different,
like when T. S. Eliot reframed the journey of the Magi
via a Beckettian landscape,
though *Godot* had not yet been written.
I am conscious of how I am referring to white-men writers
here,
to white guys alone in their rooms.
But I am so glad for those men.
I love them,
by which I mean I love their work and I am grateful they
made it.
In "Journey of the Magi," Eliot writes as one of the three
kings traveling to greet Christ.
He turns Christ's birth into a death,
that is, his own death,

the death of his beliefs,
the death of magic and astrology,
and he acknowledges how difficult this death is,
and he mourns that life, which Christ's birth marks
the ending of.
Abracadabra; annihilation.

The Chinese/English paper adds that "beginners should
select balls of a smaller size"
and then "increase ball size as one's proficiency improves."
I held the two balls in my hands gently.
The paper said ball-owners "should avoid violently
knocking them against each other and against solid objects
and surfaces."
That's what the box was for, to keep them safe.
I put them back in their bed, which is a box.
I gave the box back to my daughter.
She went off to play with them.
Those balls can't be busted.

4.

Now it is time to have pancakes.

We had them already, yes.
But now we are having them again.
We were just thinking about pancakes,
and now we can have them again.

We can have pancakes a million times,
every day of our entire lives,
like red-hot pokers applied to the spine,
we can have pancakes with syrup on them.

Let us take the carafe of maple syrup!
Let us hold it aloft!

And now:

I am going to pour syrup on my pancakes,
and then I am going to pour it on my kids',
and then I am going to pour it on the slit gong
and all the other artwork in the Met.

I am going to pour syrup on my family,
on my husband and three children,
on our apartment and our building,
on Lincoln Center and Radio City.

I am going to pour lovely maple syrup,
which is a syrup that comes from trees,
which is a sap that flows from a tree,
and which you can lick right off a tree.

You can do this by kneeling beside it
as if you are about to make love to it.
You can lick syrup from its hole,
and this is something you should do right now.

In the meantime I'll pour syrup on quilts,
and I'll pour syrup on boilermakers,
and I'll pour syrup on ballerinas,
and I'll pour syrup on mice and roaches.

I'll pour syrup on computer keyboards,
on the Talking Heads and on Tchaikovsky,
on Beckett and T. S. Eliot,
and on the status of women in publishing.

I will pour maple syrup on it all,
warmed syrup from my glass carafe,
I will pour and pour maple syrup,
and then I will eat everything,

yes, then I will eat every last thing
maple syrup ever was poured on.

5.

The·slit gongs of Vanuatu are unusual in that, unlike other
slit gongs of the region, they are played standing up.
Vertical slit gongs are found only in central Vanuatu.
Formerly, they played an important role in communication.
"Consisting of a complex system of beats and pauses whose
meaning is understood by both senders and recipients,
these languages permit messages about specific topics, even
specific individuals, to be transmitted through the densely

forested mountainous terrain at the speed of sound," wrote Kjellgren in the *Journal of Museum Ethnography*.

Slit gongs are a type of telephone.

The one on display at the Met is decorated with iconography that is particular to the tribe of the chief who commissioned it.

The tribal chief's name was Tain Mal, and this slit gong was made in the mid to late 1960s.

The slit gong depicts an ancestor of the tribe.

The ancestor has curling tusks like the ones on the pigs that are sacred to this tribe.

Each of his eyes has a red pupil, outlined in black and then embellished with a design that extends out in red, white, and green paint.

According to James Tainmal, the brother of tribal chief Tain Mal, these eye designs represent "the morning star (metan galgal)."

The meanings of the morning star are manifold for Westerners.

Astronomically, the morning star is the planet Venus when it appears in the east before sunrise.

It is also the name of a club with a heavy, spiked head.

In biblical terms, the morning star is a phrase used to refer to Satan.

In biblical terms, it is also a phrase used to refer to Jesus.

I have just about had it with words and their meanings.

I am going to call up Tchaikovsky, I mean Kafka, and complain.

6.

In our house we are not very religious.
Some days I think this is a blessing.
We celebrate Christmas every year.
We trim the tree with old toys and other castoffs.
My son's glow-in-the-dark cast from when he fractured his
wrist is on there.
And there is a naughty anime doll I found in a public toilet
in Japan.
She is half dressed and wears bunny ears; I place her deep
in the needles.
And there is a tiny stuffed tiger from my own childhood,
which I bought at the Peabody Museum in Connecticut.
It has real fur on it, and I remember thinking it was like an
object from another world.
It was as exotic to me as the stack of cards my friend's
mother kept from her husband's flower bouquets.
That man is no longer alive.
He died not long after I graduated from college.
But I like to think of that stack of cards and what would
have happened if he had lived longer,
if he had stayed a sober flower-bearer.
They would have had a stack of cards taller than their
house, then.
They would have had to keep that stack outside like a
telephone pole.
They could have made calls to the morning star with it.
Maybe I could have talked too.

We could have gotten a party line.

We could all have been singing together.

And all our singing could have been transmitted from that
stack of cards deep into space,

as if there were a great magician/telephone operator up
there

and he was like a stagehand, wearing a headset and holding
wires,

and he was plugging the wires in and taking them out,

and he was backstage, in the dark,

and he saw everything and heard everything,

and he had mercy.

7.

In the *Journal of Museum Ethnography,* Kjellgren explains
that the slit gong is used for special ceremonies in
Vanuatu.

The ceremonies are part of a male achievement system
called *fangkon,* or "sacred fire."

As an initiate passes through each stage, he rises up one
level,

gaining "religious knowledge, more social prestige, and
more say in village affairs."

Men of each *fangkon* grade cook and eat only with those of
the same grade.

Social position is not passed down but is achieved by each
individual for himself.

Each man tries to rise up through the grade system until
he reaches the pinnacle grade of *Mal*.
Kjellgren notes that "men who have achieved the highest
grades become de facto leaders of society" and that it is
"normally only older men who can muster the enormous
resources required to attain the highest grades."
"In some instances," Kjellgren adds, "certain fangkon grades
are open to women,
but only to those whose husbands have already achieved a
certain fangkon rank."

8.

This is just to say
that I have written this manuscript without a mouse.
I have a laptop that is mouseless.
It has a touchpad instead.
The touchpad is like a mini-stage;
my fingers have been mousing around on it.
I took my mouseless laptop with me recently
when my family and I went to Tampa.
We all went to visit my mother
at the assisted-living center.
There was a moment when I was in her apartment
and it was just me and her and my daughter.
It was not quite worlds colliding;
it was three generations of females.

You'd think we would have had a lot to say.
You'd think there would have been many words running
around.
Instead there were many pauses,
and the pauses were soft like a bed.
The few words that were spoken
were mostly about objects.
My mother's apartment has a lot of strange stuff in it,
and my daughter would pick something up to examine it
and then my mother would comment on it;
it was like being at the Met with a docent.
My daughter picked up an old aspirin bottle.
The label had been removed.
It was just a white plastic bottle now,
and it was filled with nickels, dimes, and pennies.
My daughter shook it like a maraca,
and then she grinned at my mother;
it was clear that she wanted this instrument.
My mother gave it to her, smiling,
and her granddaughter smiled back at her,
exclaiming, "I'm rich!"
There was probably less than a dollar in there,
which just goes to show you
that wealth is a matter of perception,
just like luck is.
We sat there, the three of us,
and ate cookies and drank tea.
We sat in the shape of a triangle.

We sat in the shape of a Christmas tree.
We were gigantic in our separate chairs.

We sat and were soft together,
and the change was spread out on the couch
and it was marveled at.

9.

My mother and the mice have arrived at Louse Point.
They have parked without the required permit.
They hope they won't get caught.
My mother is helping the mice to the beach.
It's not a very long walk, but the mice can't carry anything.
My mother is carrying the beach chairs and the blanket
and the towels and the food.
My mother still doesn't have vision in her right eye,
but she is used to it now.
She wears an eye patch like Drosselmeier.
She wears it well; it suits her.
It is going to be sunset soon.
They are going to watch the sunset and drink wine and
eat cheese.
My mother picked up a nice bottle of merlot.
She is going to drink just one glass because she is driving.
At last she gets them all settled.
They are sitting there, and the weather is perfect.
And my mother is still in her postsurgery euphoria.

She is nearly crying with joy,
and she suggests to the mice that they get married right
then and there
as she is newly vested with the power to perform their
marriage.
She shows them the certificate she got off the internet.
And the mice laugh happily and agree to this plan,
and my mother stands to say the words.
She is about to intone the sacred marrying words,
and her black eye patch is ablaze like a comet,
when the drunken cockroach drives up in the gallbladder-
car and remembers them, though they don't remember
him.
And he walks onto the beach and is overcome by the sight
of them,
and my mother, whom he remembers as older and frailer,
is now bright like a spotlight on Broadway.
She is standing there in her simple cotton dress,
looking like the girl Jackson Pollock she was on the farm,
only with an eye patch,
and the cockroach is stunned by her beauty
and also by his own remorse.
And he knows that he can't return to that moment
on the road in the department store.
He can never return to that road.
That magic show is long gone.
Everything becomes awake,
one word turns into another,
everything becomes a wake,

and he steps up and offers to be their witness, which they
had forgotten they needed.
And he stands there silent like a slit gong in a museum
as the mice are married by my mother.
And then they all sit down together and eat and drink.
And it is quiet with the sound of the ocean, which
is almost but not quite like cowbells, triangles, and
glockenspiels.
And when it gets dark, my mother and the cockroach
build a fire together out of driftwood,
and later, they all sleep in the *Construction,*
which is just a construction now,
because it's in a different world,
a world enlarged by challenging encounters.
It's like my mouse-mother, Louise Bourgeois,
cradling her penis *Fillette* in her arms,
or like the slit gong from Vanuatu
in the gallery in the Met,
taking a walk down Fifth Avenue
and getting in a cab to JFK
and flying back home to be hit with wooden mallets,
to stand there on the ceremonial dancing ground,
to have been a tree rooted in the earth,
and to be taken out of the ground and made into a slit
gong,
and now to be a slit gong standing among other slit gongs,
to be struck as the dancers whirl,
to be at the center of a holiday party
with all the food and sacred pigs.

To see it all at once like in a mirror,
to be in one world and to multiply,
to be in one world and remember a mother,
to be in one world
and to hold all the others.

RESOURCES

Berkow, Ira. "Joe Louis Was There Earlier." *New York Times,* April 22, 1997. http://www.nytimes.com/1997/04/22/sports/joe-louis-was-there-earlier.html.

Bleiler, E. F. Introduction to *The Best Tales of Hoffmann,* by E. T. A. Hoffmann, xxiv. New York: Dover, 1967.

Bourgeois, Louise. *Destruction of the Father, Reconstruction of the Father: Writings and Interviews, 1923–1997.* Edited by Marie-Laure Bernadac and Hans-Ulrich Obrist. London: Violette Editions, 1998.

Fisher, Jennifer. *Nutcracker Nation.* New Haven, CT: Yale University Press, 2003.

Hoffmann, E. T. A. *Weird Tales,* trans. and biographical memoir by J. T. Bealby. New York: Charles Scribner's Sons, 1885.

Kaufman, Sarah. "Breaking Pointe: 'The Nutcracker' Takes More than It Gives to World of Ballet." *Washington Post,* November 22, 2009. https://www.washingtonpost.com/wp-dyn/content/article/2009/11/20/AR2009112000316.html.

Kjellgren, Eric. "From Fanla to New York and Back: Recovering the Authorship and Iconography of a Slit Drum from Ambrym Island, Vanuatu." *Journal of Museum Ethnography* 17 (2005): 118–29.

Kourlas, Gia. "It's a Blizzard Onstage. Here's All the Dirt." *New York Times,* December 13, 2016. https://www .nytimes.com/2016/12/13/arts/dance/its-a-blizzard -onstage-heres-all-the-dirt-mark-morris-the-hart-nut -balanchine-the-nutcracker.html.

Langston, Brett, et al. "Iolanta." Tchaikovsky Research. Last modified December 24, 2016. http://en.tchaikovsky -research.net/index.php?title=Iolanta&oldid=99372.

Metropolitan Museum of Art. *Slit Gong (Atingting kon).* Accessed February 9, 2017. http://www.metmuseum .org/collection/the-collection-online/search/309995.

Moscow Ballet. "History of *The Nutcracker.*" Accessed February 9, 2017. http://www.nutcracker.com/about -mb/history-of-nutcracker.

North Carolina Academy of Dance Arts Online. "The History of *The Nutcracker.*" Accessed June 5, 2017. http://www.danceacademyofnc.com/default.cfm ?fa=nutcrackerhistory.

NPR Staff. "No Sugar Plums Here: The Dark, Romantic Roots of *The Nutcracker.*" *All Things Considered.* National Public Radio. Aired December 25, 2012. http://www.npr.org/2012/12/25/167732828/no -sugar-plums-here-the-dark-romantic-roots-of-the -nutcracker.

Parson, Annie-B. "An Interview with Choreographer, Dancer and Director Annie-B Parson." By Amy Fusselman. *Ohio Edit* October 4, 2016. http://ohioedit .com/2016/10/04/an-interview-with-choreographer -and-director-annie-b-parson.

Spice, Nicholas. "Winnicott and Music." In *The Elusive Child,* edited by Lesley Caldwell. London: Karnac Books, 2004.

ACKNOWLEDGMENTS

Thank you so much for your support of this project: Elisa Albert, Donnie Boman, Dave Eggers, Anastasia Higginbotham, Molly MacDermot, Sarah Manguso, Spike Medernach, Alma Micic, Leigh Newman, Annie-B Parson, Elena Passarello, Ali Rachel Pearl, Melissa Robbins, Walter Robinson, Tracy Roe, Heather Sellers, Joshua Wolf Shenk, Nicholas Spice, Gilmore Tamny, Lauren Wein, and Matvei Yankelevich.

Thank you to the wonderful crew at Coffee House Press, especially Caroline Casey, Lizzie Davis, Chris Fischbach, and Carla Valadez. Thanks also to cover designer Kyle G. Hunter.

Thank you to my husband, Frank, and my children, King, Mick, and Katie.

I am grateful to Jennifer Fisher for her book *Nutcracker Nation* and encourage those interested in the ballet to read it.

Coffee House Press began as a small letterpress operation in 1972 and has grown into an internationally renowned nonprofit publisher of literary fiction, essay, poetry, and other work that doesn't fit neatly into genre categories.

Coffee House is both a publisher and an arts organization. Through our *Books in Action* program and publications, we've become interdisciplinary collaborators and incubators for new work and audience experiences. Our vision for the future is one where a publisher is a catalyst and connector.

LITERATURE
is not the same thing as
PUBLISHING

FUNDER ACKNOWLEDGMENTS

Coffee House Press is an internationally renowned independent book publisher and arts nonprofit based in Minneapolis, MN; through its literary publications and *Books in Action* program, Coffee House acts as a catalyst and connector—between authors and readers, ideas and resources, creativity and community, inspiration and action.

Coffee House Press books are made possible through the generous support of grants and donations from corporations, state and federal grant programs, family foundations, and the many individuals who believe in the transformational power of literature. This activity is made possible by the voters of Minnesota through a Minnesota State Arts Board Operating Support grant, thanks to the legislative appropriation from the arts and cultural heritage fund. Coffee House also receives major operating support from the Amazon Literary Partnership, the Jerome Foundation, The McKnight Foundation, Target Foundation, and the National Endowment for the Arts (NEA). To find out more about how NEA grants impact individuals and communities, visit www.arts.gov.

Coffee House Press receives additional support from the Elmer L. & Eleanor J. Andersen Foundation; the David & Mary Anderson Family Foundation; the Buuck Family Foundation; Fredrikson & Byron, P.A.; Dorsey & Whitney LLP; the Fringe Foundation; Kenneth Koch Literary Estate; the Knight Foundation; the Matching Grant Program Fund of the Minneapolis Foundation; Mr. Pancks' Fund in memory of Graham Kimpton; the Schwab Charitable Fund; Schwegman, Lundberg & Woessner, P.A.; the U.S. Bank Foundation; and VSA Minnesota for the Metropolitan Regional Arts Council.

THE PUBLISHER'S CIRCLE OF COFFEE HOUSE PRESS

Publisher's Circle members make significant contributions to Coffee House Press's annual giving campaign. Understanding that a strong financial base is necessary for the press to meet the challenges and opportunities that arise each year, this group plays a crucial part in the success of Coffee House's mission.

Recent Publisher's Circle members include many anonymous donors, Suzanne Allen, Patricia A. Beithon, the E. Thomas Binger & Rebecca Rand Fund of the Minneapolis Foundation, Andrew Brantingham, Robert & Gail Buuck, Claire Casey, Louise Copeland, Jane Dalrymple-Hollo, Mary Ebert & Paul Stembler, Kaywin Feldman & Jim Lutz, Chris Fischbach & Katie Dublinski, Sally French, Jocelyn Hale & Glenn Miller, the Rehael Fund-Roger Hale/Nor Hall of the Minneapolis Foundation, Randy Hartten & Ron Lotz, Dylan Hicks & Nina Hale, William Hardacker, Randall Heath, Jeffrey Hom, Carl & Heidi Horsch, Amy L. Hubbard & Geoffrey J. Kehoe Fund, Kenneth Kahn & Susan Dicker, Stephen & Isabel Keating, Kenneth Koch Literary Estate, Cinda Kornblum, Jennifer Kwon Dobbs & Stefan Liess, Lambert Family Foundation, Lenfestey Family Foundation, Sarah Lutman & Rob Rudolph, the Carol & Aaron Mack Charitable Fund of the Minneapolis Foundation, George & Olga Mack, Joshua Mack & Ron Warren, Gillian McCain, Malcolm S. McDermid & Katie Windle, Mary & Malcolm McDermid, Sjur Midness & Briar Andresen, Maureen Millea Smith & Daniel Smith, Peter Nelson & Jennifer Swenson, Enrique & Jennifer Olivarez, Alan Polsky, Marc Porter & James Hennessy, Robin Preble, Alexis Scott, Ruth Stricker Dayton, Jeffrey Sugerman & Sarah Schultz, Nan G. & Stephen C. Swid, Kenneth Thorp in memory of Allan Kornblum & Rochelle Ratner, Patricia Tilton, Joanne Von Blon, Stu Wilson & Melissa Barker, Warren D. Woessner & Iris C. Freeman, Margaret Wurtele, and Wayne P. Zink & Christopher Schout.

For more information about the Publisher's Circle and other ways to support Coffee House Press books, authors, and activities, please visit www.coffeehousepress.org/support or contact us at info@coffeehousepress.org.

AMY FUSSELMAN is the author of three previous books of nonfiction. She lives in Manhattan with her husband and three children.

Idiophone was designed by
Bookmobile Design & Digital Publisher Services.
Text is set in Arno Pro.